The Absolute Best

Address Book and Journal

For You

Activinotes

Activinotes

DAILY JOURNALS, PLANNERS, NOTEBOOKS AND OTHER BLANK BOOKS

Address Book

name : _____
address : _____
_____
_____
mobile 1 #: _____
mobile 2 #: _____
work #: _____
home #: _____
email :_____
birthday : _____

name : _____
address : _____
_____
_____
mobile 1 #: _____
mobile 2 #: _____
work #: _____
home #: _____
email :_____
birthday : _____

name : _____
address : _____
_____
_____
mobile 1 #: _____
mobile 2 #: _____
work #: _____
home #: _____
email :_____
birthday : _____

name : _____
address : _____
_____
_____
mobile 1 #: _____
mobile 2 #: _____
work #: _____
home #: _____
email :_____
birthday : _____

name : _____
address : _____
_____
_____
mobile 1 #: _____
mobile 2 #: _____
work #: _____
home #: _____
email :_____
birthday : _____

name : _____
address : _____
_____
_____
mobile 1 #: _____
mobile 2 #: _____
work #: _____
home #: _____
email :_____
birthday : _____

Address Book

name : _____
address : _____
_____
_____
mobile 1 #: _____
mobile 2 #: _____
work #: _____
home #: _____
email : _____
birthday : _____

name : _____
address : _____
_____
_____
mobile 1 #: _____
mobile 2 #: _____
work #: _____
home #: _____
email : _____
birthday : _____

name : _____
address : _____
_____
_____
mobile 1 #: _____
mobile 2 #: _____
work #: _____
home #: _____
email : _____
birthday : _____

name : _____
address : _____
_____
_____
mobile 1 #: _____
mobile 2 #: _____
work #: _____
home #: _____
email : _____
birthday : _____

name : _____
address : _____
_____
_____
mobile 1 #: _____
mobile 2 #: _____
work #: _____
home #: _____
email : _____
birthday : _____

name : _____
address : _____
_____
_____
mobile 1 #: _____
mobile 2 #: _____
work #: _____
home #: _____
email : _____
birthday : _____

journal

Address Book

name : _____
address : _____
_____
_____

mobile 1 #: _____
mobile 2 #: _____
work #: _____
home #: _____

email : _____
birthday : _____

name : _____
address : _____
_____
_____

mobile 1 #: _____
mobile 2 #: _____
work #: _____
home #: _____

email : _____
birthday : _____

name : _____
address : _____
_____
_____

mobile 1 #: _____
mobile 2 #: _____
work #: _____
home #: _____

email : _____
birthday : _____

name : _____
address : _____
_____
_____

mobile 1 #: _____
mobile 2 #: _____
work #: _____
home #: _____

email : _____
birthday : _____

name : _____
address : _____
_____
_____

mobile 1 #: _____
mobile 2 #: _____
work #: _____
home #: _____

email : _____
birthday : _____

name : _____
address : _____
_____
_____

mobile 1 #: _____
mobile 2 #: _____
work #: _____
home #: _____

email : _____
birthday : _____

 journal

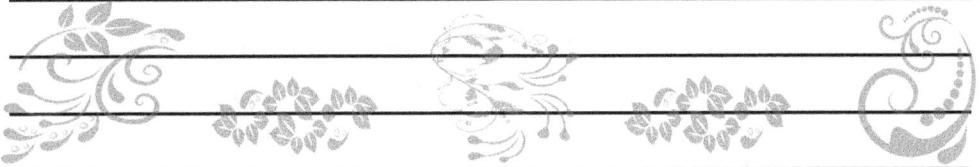

Address Book

name : _____
address : _____
_____
_____
mobile 1 #: _____
mobile 2 #: _____
work #: _____
home #: _____
email :_____
birthday : _____

name : _____
address : _____
_____
_____
mobile 1 #: _____
mobile 2 #: _____
work #: _____
home #: _____
email :_____
birthday : _____

name : _____
address : _____
_____
_____
mobile 1 #: _____
mobile 2 #: _____
work #: _____
home #: _____
email :_____
birthday : _____

name : _____
address : _____
_____
_____
mobile 1 #: _____
mobile 2 #: _____
work #: _____
home #: _____
email :_____
birthday : _____

name : _____
address : _____
_____
_____
mobile 1 #: _____
mobile 2 #: _____
work #: _____
home #: _____
email :_____
birthday : _____

name : _____
address : _____
_____
_____
mobile 1 #: _____
mobile 2 #: _____
work #: _____
home #: _____
email :_____
birthday : _____

 journal

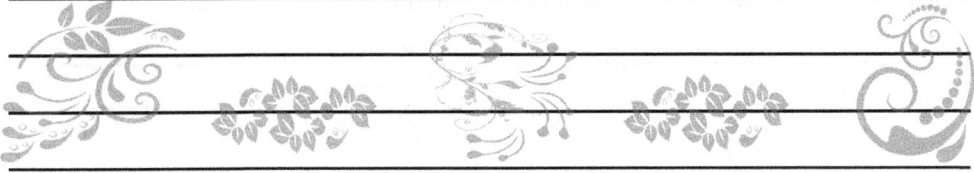

Address Book

name : _____
address : _____
_____
_____
mobile 1 #: _____
mobile 2 #: _____
work #: _____
home #: _____
email : _____
birthday : _____

name : _____
address : _____
_____
_____
mobile 1 #: _____
mobile 2 #: _____
work #: _____
home #: _____
email : _____
birthday : _____

name : _____
address : _____
_____
_____
mobile 1 #: _____
mobile 2 #: _____
work #: _____
home #: _____
email : _____
birthday : _____

name : _____
address : _____
_____
_____
mobile 1 #: _____
mobile 2 #: _____
work #: _____
home #: _____
email : _____
birthday : _____

name : _____
address : _____
_____
_____
mobile 1 #: _____
mobile 2 #: _____
work #: _____
home #: _____
email : _____
birthday : _____

name : _____
address : _____
_____
_____
mobile 1 #: _____
mobile 2 #: _____
work #: _____
home #: _____
email : _____
birthday : _____

journal

Address Book

name : _____
address : _____
_____
_____
mobile 1 #: _____
mobile 2 #: _____
work #: _____
home #: _____
email :_____
birthday : _____

name : _____
address : _____
_____
_____
mobile 1 #: _____
mobile 2 #: _____
work #: _____
home #: _____
email :_____
birthday : _____

name : _____
address : _____
_____
_____
mobile 1 #: _____
mobile 2 #: _____
work #: _____
home #: _____
email :_____
birthday : _____

name : _____
address : _____
_____
_____
mobile 1 #: _____
mobile 2 #: _____
work #: _____
home #: _____
email :_____
birthday : _____

name : _____
address : _____
_____
_____
mobile 1 #: _____
mobile 2 #: _____
work #: _____
home #: _____
email :_____
birthday : _____

name : _____
address : _____
_____
_____
mobile 1 #: _____
mobile 2 #: _____
work #: _____
home #: _____
email :_____
birthday : _____

 journal

Address Book

name : _____
address : _____
_____
_____
mobile 1 #: _____
mobile 2 #: _____
work #: _____
home #: _____
email : _____
birthday : _____

name : _____
address : _____
_____
_____
mobile 1 #: _____
mobile 2 #: _____
work #: _____
home #: _____
email : _____
birthday : _____

name : _____
address : _____
_____
_____
mobile 1 #: _____
mobile 2 #: _____
work #: _____
home #: _____
email : _____
birthday : _____

name : _____
address : _____
_____
_____
mobile 1 #: _____
mobile 2 #: _____
work #: _____
home #: _____
email : _____
birthday : _____

name : _____
address : _____
_____
_____
mobile 1 #: _____
mobile 2 #: _____
work #: _____
home #: _____
email : _____
birthday : _____

name : _____
address : _____
_____
_____
mobile 1 #: _____
mobile 2 #: _____
work #: _____
home #: _____
email : _____
birthday : _____

 journal

Address Book

name : _____
address : _____
_____
_____
mobile 1 #: _____
mobile 2 #: _____
work #: _____
home #: _____
email :_____
birthday : _____

name : _____
address : _____
_____
_____
mobile 1 #: _____
mobile 2 #: _____
work #: _____
home #: _____
email :_____
birthday : _____

name : _____
address : _____
_____
_____
mobile 1 #: _____
mobile 2 #: _____
work #: _____
home #: _____
email :_____
birthday : _____

name : _____
address : _____
_____
_____
mobile 1 #: _____
mobile 2 #: _____
work #: _____
home #: _____
email :_____
birthday : _____

name : _____
address : _____
_____
_____
mobile 1 #: _____
mobile 2 #: _____
work #: _____
home #: _____
email :_____
birthday : _____

name : _____
address : _____
_____
_____
mobile 1 #: _____
mobile 2 #: _____
work #: _____
home #: _____
email :_____
birthday : _____

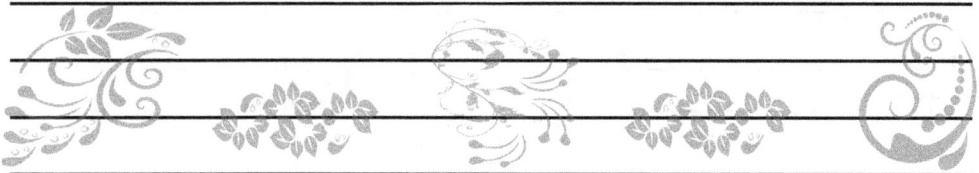

Address Book

name : _____
address : _____
_____
_____
mobile 1 #: _____
mobile 2 #: _____
work #: _____
home #: _____
email : _____
birthday : _____

name : _____
address : _____
_____
_____
mobile 1 #: _____
mobile 2 #: _____
work #: _____
home #: _____
email : _____
birthday : _____

name : _____
address : _____
_____
_____
mobile 1 #: _____
mobile 2 #: _____
work #: _____
home #: _____
email : _____
birthday : _____

name : _____
address : _____
_____
_____
mobile 1 #: _____
mobile 2 #: _____
work #: _____
home #: _____
email : _____
birthday : _____

name : _____
address : _____
_____
_____
mobile 1 #: _____
mobile 2 #: _____
work #: _____
home #: _____
email : _____
birthday : _____

name : _____
address : _____
_____
_____
mobile 1 #: _____
mobile 2 #: _____
work #: _____
home #: _____
email : _____
birthday : _____

 journal

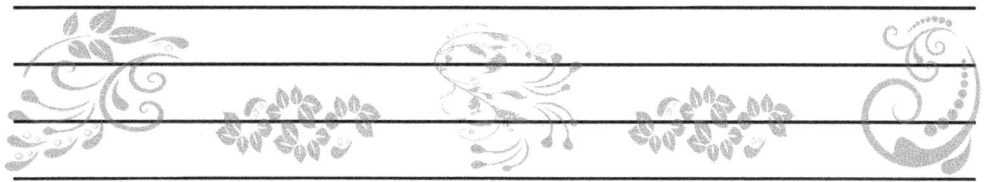

Address Book

name : _____
address : _____
_____
_____
mobile 1 #: _____
mobile 2 #: _____
work #: _____
home #: _____
email : _____
birthday : _____

name : _____
address : _____
_____
_____
mobile 1 #: _____
mobile 2 #: _____
work #: _____
home #: _____
email : _____
birthday : _____

name : _____
address : _____
_____
_____
mobile 1 #: _____
mobile 2 #: _____
work #: _____
home #: _____
email : _____
birthday : _____

name : _____
address : _____
_____
_____
mobile 1 #: _____
mobile 2 #: _____
work #: _____
home #: _____
email : _____
birthday : _____

name : _____
address : _____
_____
_____
mobile 1 #: _____
mobile 2 #: _____
work #: _____
home #: _____
email : _____
birthday : _____

name : _____
address : _____
_____
_____
mobile 1 #: _____
mobile 2 #: _____
work #: _____
home #: _____
email : _____
birthday : _____

 journal

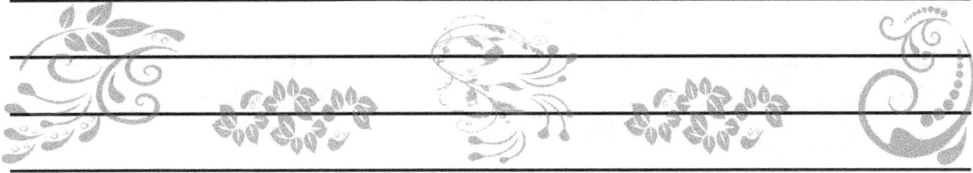

Address Book

name : _____
address : _____
_____
_____

mobile 1 #: _____
mobile 2 #: _____
work #: _____
home #: _____

email : _____
birthday : _____

name : _____
address : _____
_____
_____

mobile 1 #: _____
mobile 2 #: _____
work #: _____
home #: _____

email : _____
birthday : _____

name : _____
address : _____
_____
_____

mobile 1 #: _____
mobile 2 #: _____
work #: _____
home #: _____

email : _____
birthday : _____

name : _____
address : _____
_____
_____

mobile 1 #: _____
mobile 2 #: _____
work #: _____
home #: _____

email : _____
birthday : _____

name : _____
address : _____
_____
_____

mobile 1 #: _____
mobile 2 #: _____
work #: _____
home #: _____

email : _____
birthday : _____

name : _____
address : _____
_____
_____

mobile 1 #: _____
mobile 2 #: _____
work #: _____
home #: _____

email : _____
birthday : _____

journal

Address Book

name : _____
address : _____
_____
_____
mobile 1 #: _____
mobile 2 #: _____
work #: _____
home #: _____
email :_____
birthday : _____

name : _____
address : _____
_____
_____
mobile 1 #: _____
mobile 2 #: _____
work #: _____
home #: _____
email :_____
birthday : _____

name : _____
address : _____
_____
_____
mobile 1 #: _____
mobile 2 #: _____
work #: _____
home #: _____
email :_____
birthday : _____

name : _____
address : _____
_____
_____
mobile 1 #: _____
mobile 2 #: _____
work #: _____
home #: _____
email :_____
birthday : _____

name : _____
address : _____
_____
_____
mobile 1 #: _____
mobile 2 #: _____
work #: _____
home #: _____
email :_____
birthday : _____

name : _____
address : _____
_____
_____
mobile 1 #: _____
mobile 2 #: _____
work #: _____
home #: _____
email :_____
birthday : _____

 journal

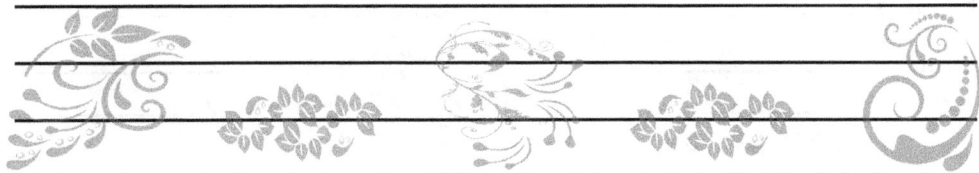

Address Book

name : _____
address : _____
_____
_____
mobile 1 #: _____
mobile 2 #: _____
work #: _____
home #: _____
email : _____
birthday : _____

name : _____
address : _____
_____
_____
mobile 1 #: _____
mobile 2 #: _____
work #: _____
home #: _____
email : _____
birthday : _____

name : _____
address : _____
_____
_____
mobile 1 #: _____
mobile 2 #: _____
work #: _____
home #: _____
email : _____
birthday : _____

name : _____
address : _____
_____
_____
mobile 1 #: _____
mobile 2 #: _____
work #: _____
home #: _____
email : _____
birthday : _____

name : _____
address : _____
_____
_____
mobile 1 #: _____
mobile 2 #: _____
work #: _____
home #: _____
email : _____
birthday : _____

name : _____
address : _____
_____
_____
mobile 1 #: _____
mobile 2 #: _____
work #: _____
home #: _____
email : _____
birthday : _____

Address Book

name : _____
address : _____
_____
_____
mobile 1 #: _____
mobile 2 #: _____
work #: _____
home #: _____
email :_____
birthday : _____

name : _____
address : _____
_____
_____
mobile 1 #: _____
mobile 2 #: _____
work #: _____
home #: _____
email :_____
birthday : _____

name : _____
address : _____
_____
_____
mobile 1 #: _____
mobile 2 #: _____
work #: _____
home #: _____
email :_____
birthday : _____

name : _____
address : _____
_____
_____
mobile 1 #: _____
mobile 2 #: _____
work #: _____
home #: _____
email :_____
birthday : _____

name : _____
address : _____
_____
_____
mobile 1 #: _____
mobile 2 #: _____
work #: _____
home #: _____
email :_____
birthday : _____

name : _____
address : _____
_____
_____
mobile 1 #: _____
mobile 2 #: _____
work #: _____
home #: _____
email :_____
birthday : _____

 journal

Address Book

name : _____
address : _____
_____
_____

mobile 1 #: _____
mobile 2 #: _____
work #: _____
home #: _____

email : _____
birthday : _____

---

name : _____
address : _____
_____
_____

mobile 1 #: _____
mobile 2 #: _____
work #: _____
home #: _____

email : _____
birthday : _____

---

name : _____
address : _____
_____
_____

mobile 1 #: _____
mobile 2 #: _____
work #: _____
home #: _____

email : _____
birthday : _____

---

name : _____
address : _____
_____
_____

mobile 1 #: _____
mobile 2 #: _____
work #: _____
home #: _____

email : _____
birthday : _____

---

name : _____
address : _____
_____
_____

mobile 1 #: _____
mobile 2 #: _____
work #: _____
home #: _____

email : _____
birthday : _____

---

name : _____
address : _____
_____
_____

mobile 1 #: _____
mobile 2 #: _____
work #: _____
home #: _____

email : _____
birthday : _____

journal

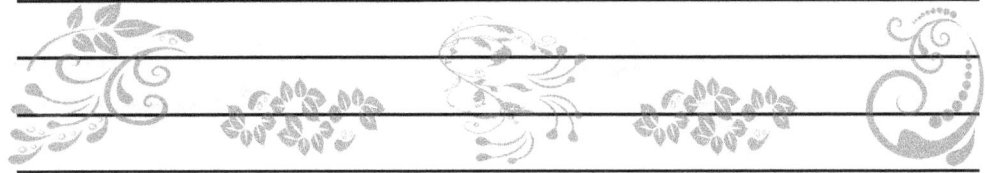

Address Book

name : _____
address : _____
_____
_____
mobile 1 #: _____
mobile 2 #: _____
work #: _____
home #: _____
email :_____
birthday : _____

name : _____
address : _____
_____
_____
mobile 1 #: _____
mobile 2 #: _____
work #: _____
home #: _____
email :_____
birthday : _____

name : _____
address : _____
_____
_____
mobile 1 #: _____
mobile 2 #: _____
work #: _____
home #: _____
email :_____
birthday : _____

name : _____
address : _____
_____
_____
mobile 1 #: _____
mobile 2 #: _____
work #: _____
home #: _____
email :_____
birthday : _____

name : _____
address : _____
_____
_____
mobile 1 #: _____
mobile 2 #: _____
work #: _____
home #: _____
email :_____
birthday : _____

name : _____
address : _____
_____
_____
mobile 1 #: _____
mobile 2 #: _____
work #: _____
home #: _____
email :_____
birthday : _____

 journal

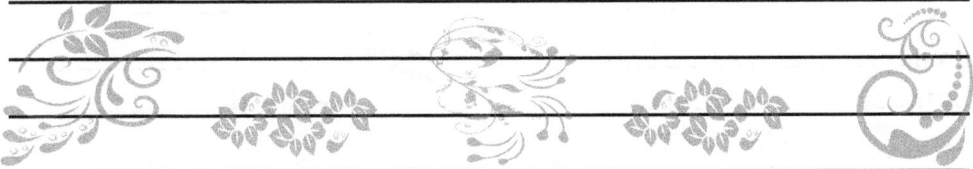

Address Book

name : _____
address : _____
_____
_____
mobile 1 #: _____
mobile 2 #: _____
work #: _____
home #: _____
email :_____
birthday : _____

name : _____
address : _____
_____
_____
mobile 1 #: _____
mobile 2 #: _____
work #: _____
home #: _____
email :_____
birthday : _____

name : _____
address : _____
_____
_____
mobile 1 #: _____
mobile 2 #: _____
work #: _____
home #: _____
email :_____
birthday : _____

name : _____
address : _____
_____
_____
mobile 1 #: _____
mobile 2 #: _____
work #: _____
home #: _____
email :_____
birthday : _____

name : _____
address : _____
_____
_____
mobile 1 #: _____
mobile 2 #: _____
work #: _____
home #: _____
email :_____
birthday : _____

name : _____
address : _____
_____
_____
mobile 1 #: _____
mobile 2 #: _____
work #: _____
home #: _____
email :_____
birthday : _____

 journal

Address Book

name : _____
address : _____
_____
_____
mobile 1 #: _____
mobile 2 #: _____
work #: _____
home #: _____
email : _____
birthday : _____

name : _____
address : _____
_____
_____
mobile 1 #: _____
mobile 2 #: _____
work #: _____
home #: _____
email : _____
birthday : _____

name : _____
address : _____
_____
_____
mobile 1 #: _____
mobile 2 #: _____
work #: _____
home #: _____
email : _____
birthday : _____

name : _____
address : _____
_____
_____
mobile 1 #: _____
mobile 2 #: _____
work #: _____
home #: _____
email : _____
birthday : _____

name : _____
address : _____
_____
_____
mobile 1 #: _____
mobile 2 #: _____
work #: _____
home #: _____
email : _____
birthday : _____

name : _____
address : _____
_____
_____
mobile 1 #: _____
mobile 2 #: _____
work #: _____
home #: _____
email : _____
birthday : _____

 journal

Address Book

name : _____
address : _____
_____
_____
mobile 1 #: _____
mobile 2 #: _____
work #: _____
home #: _____
email : _____
birthday : _____

name : _____
address : _____
_____
_____
mobile 1 #: _____
mobile 2 #: _____
work #: _____
home #: _____
email : _____
birthday : _____

name : _____
address : _____
_____
_____
mobile 1 #: _____
mobile 2 #: _____
work #: _____
home #: _____
email : _____
birthday : _____

name : _____
address : _____
_____
_____
mobile 1 #: _____
mobile 2 #: _____
work #: _____
home #: _____
email : _____
birthday : _____

name : _____
address : _____
_____
_____
mobile 1 #: _____
mobile 2 #: _____
work #: _____
home #: _____
email : _____
birthday : _____

name : _____
address : _____
_____
_____
mobile 1 #: _____
mobile 2 #: _____
work #: _____
home #: _____
email : _____
birthday : _____

 journal

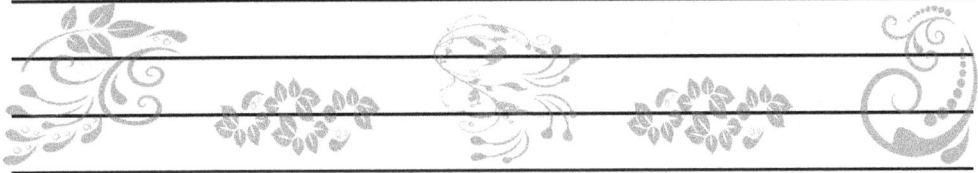

Address Book

name : _____
address : _____
_____
_____
mobile 1 #: _____
mobile 2 #: _____
work #: _____
home #: _____
email : _____
birthday : _____

name : _____
address : _____
_____
_____
mobile 1 #: _____
mobile 2 #: _____
work #: _____
home #: _____
email : _____
birthday : _____

name : _____
address : _____
_____
_____
mobile 1 #: _____
mobile 2 #: _____
work #: _____
home #: _____
email : _____
birthday : _____

name : _____
address : _____
_____
_____
mobile 1 #: _____
mobile 2 #: _____
work #: _____
home #: _____
email : _____
birthday : _____

name : _____
address : _____
_____
_____
mobile 1 #: _____
mobile 2 #: _____
work #: _____
home #: _____
email : _____
birthday : _____

name : _____
address : _____
_____
_____
mobile 1 #: _____
mobile 2 #: _____
work #: _____
home #: _____
email : _____
birthday : _____

 journal

Address Book

name : _____
address : _____
_____
_____
mobile 1 #: _____
mobile 2 #: _____
work #: _____
home #: _____
email :_____
birthday : _____

name : _____
address : _____
_____
_____
mobile 1 #: _____
mobile 2 #: _____
work #: _____
home #: _____
email : _____
birthday : _____

name : _____
address : _____
_____
_____
mobile 1 #: _____
mobile 2 #: _____
work #: _____
home #: _____
email :_____
birthday : _____

name : _____
address : _____
_____
_____
mobile 1 #: _____
mobile 2 #: _____
work #: _____
home #: _____
email : _____
birthday : _____

name : _____
address : _____
_____
_____
mobile 1 #: _____
mobile 2 #: _____
work #: _____
home #: _____
email :_____
birthday : _____

name : _____
address : _____
_____
_____
mobile 1 #: _____
mobile 2 #: _____
work #: _____
home #: _____
email : _____
birthday : _____

 journal

Address Book

name : _____
address : _____
_____
_____
mobile 1 #: _____
mobile 2 #: _____
work #: _____
home #: _____
email : _____
birthday : _____

name : _____
address : _____
_____
_____
mobile 1 #: _____
mobile 2 #: _____
work #: _____
home #: _____
email : _____
birthday : _____

name : _____
address : _____
_____
_____
mobile 1 #: _____
mobile 2 #: _____
work #: _____
home #: _____
email : _____
birthday : _____

name : _____
address : _____
_____
_____
mobile 1 #: _____
mobile 2 #: _____
work #: _____
home #: _____
email : _____
birthday : _____

name : _____
address : _____
_____
_____
mobile 1 #: _____
mobile 2 #: _____
work #: _____
home #: _____
email : _____
birthday : _____

name : _____
address : _____
_____
_____
mobile 1 #: _____
mobile 2 #: _____
work #: _____
home #: _____
email : _____
birthday : _____

 journal

Address Book

name : _____
address : _____
_____
_____

mobile 1 #: _____
mobile 2 #: _____
work #: _____
home #: _____

email : _____
birthday : _____

name : _____
address : _____
_____
_____

mobile 1 #: _____
mobile 2 #: _____
work #: _____
home #: _____

email : _____
birthday : _____

name : _____
address : _____
_____
_____

mobile 1 #: _____
mobile 2 #: _____
work #: _____
home #: _____

email : _____
birthday : _____

name : _____
address : _____
_____
_____

mobile 1 #: _____
mobile 2 #: _____
work #: _____
home #: _____

email : _____
birthday : _____

name : _____
address : _____
_____
_____

mobile 1 #: _____
mobile 2 #: _____
work #: _____
home #: _____

email : _____
birthday : _____

name : _____
address : _____
_____
_____

mobile 1 #: _____
mobile 2 #: _____
work #: _____
home #: _____

email : _____
birthday : _____

journal

Address Book

name : _____
address : _____
_____
_____
mobile 1 #: _____
mobile 2 #: _____
work #: _____
home #: _____
email : _____
birthday : _____

name : _____
address : _____
_____
_____
mobile 1 #: _____
mobile 2 #: _____
work #: _____
home #: _____
email : _____
birthday : _____

name : _____
address : _____
_____
_____
mobile 1 #: _____
mobile 2 #: _____
work #: _____
home #: _____
email : _____
birthday : _____

name : _____
address : _____
_____
_____
mobile 1 #: _____
mobile 2 #: _____
work #: _____
home #: _____
email : _____
birthday : _____

name : _____
address : _____
_____
_____
mobile 1 #: _____
mobile 2 #: _____
work #: _____
home #: _____
email : _____
birthday : _____

name : _____
address : _____
_____
_____
mobile 1 #: _____
mobile 2 #: _____
work #: _____
home #: _____
email : _____
birthday : _____

 journal

Address Book

name : _____
address : _____
_____
_____
mobile 1 #: _____
mobile 2 #: _____
work #: _____
home #: _____
email : _____
birthday : _____

name : _____
address : _____
_____
_____
mobile 1 #: _____
mobile 2 #: _____
work #: _____
home #: _____
email : _____
birthday : _____

name : _____
address : _____
_____
_____
mobile 1 #: _____
mobile 2 #: _____
work #: _____
home #: _____
email : _____
birthday : _____

name : _____
address : _____
_____
_____
mobile 1 #: _____
mobile 2 #: _____
work #: _____
home #: _____
email : _____
birthday : _____

name : _____
address : _____
_____
_____
mobile 1 #: _____
mobile 2 #: _____
work #: _____
home #: _____
email : _____
birthday : _____

name : _____
address : _____
_____
_____
mobile 1 #: _____
mobile 2 #: _____
work #: _____
home #: _____
email : _____
birthday : _____

 journal

Address Book

name : _____
address : _____
_____
_____

mobile 1 #: _____
mobile 2 #: _____
work #: _____
home #: _____

email :_____
birthday : _____

name : _____
address : _____
_____
_____

mobile 1 #: _____
mobile 2 #: _____
work #: _____
home #: _____

email :_____
birthday : _____

name : _____
address : _____
_____
_____

mobile 1 #: _____
mobile 2 #: _____
work #: _____
home #: _____

email :_____
birthday : _____

name : _____
address : _____
_____
_____

mobile 1 #: _____
mobile 2 #: _____
work #: _____
home #: _____

email :_____
birthday : _____

name : _____
address : _____
_____
_____

mobile 1 #: _____
mobile 2 #: _____
work #: _____
home #: _____

email :_____
birthday : _____

name : _____
address : _____
_____
_____

mobile 1 #: _____
mobile 2 #: _____
work #: _____
home #: _____

email :_____
birthday : _____

 journal

Address Book

name : _____
address : _____
_____
_____
mobile 1 #: _____
mobile 2 #: _____
work #: _____
home #: _____
email : _____
birthday : _____

name : _____
address : _____
_____
_____
mobile 1 #: _____
mobile 2 #: _____
work #: _____
home #: _____
email : _____
birthday : _____

name : _____
address : _____
_____
_____
mobile 1 #: _____
mobile 2 #: _____
work #: _____
home #: _____
email : _____
birthday : _____

name : _____
address : _____
_____
_____
mobile 1 #: _____
mobile 2 #: _____
work #: _____
home #: _____
email : _____
birthday : _____

name : _____
address : _____
_____
_____
mobile 1 #: _____
mobile 2 #: _____
work #: _____
home #: _____
email : _____
birthday : _____

name : _____
address : _____
_____
_____
mobile 1 #: _____
mobile 2 #: _____
work #: _____
home #: _____
email : _____
birthday : _____

 journal

Address Book

name : _____
address : _____
_____
_____
mobile 1 #: _____
mobile 2 #: _____
work #: _____
home #: _____
email : _____
birthday : _____

name : _____
address : _____
_____
_____
mobile 1 #: _____
mobile 2 #: _____
work #: _____
home #: _____
email : _____
birthday : _____

name : _____
address : _____
_____
_____
mobile 1 #: _____
mobile 2 #: _____
work #: _____
home #: _____
email : _____
birthday : _____

name : _____
address : _____
_____
_____
mobile 1 #: _____
mobile 2 #: _____
work #: _____
home #: _____
email : _____
birthday : _____

name : _____
address : _____
_____
_____
mobile 1 #: _____
mobile 2 #: _____
work #: _____
home #: _____
email : _____
birthday : _____

name : _____
address : _____
_____
_____
mobile 1 #: _____
mobile 2 #: _____
work #: _____
home #: _____
email : _____
birthday : _____

 journal

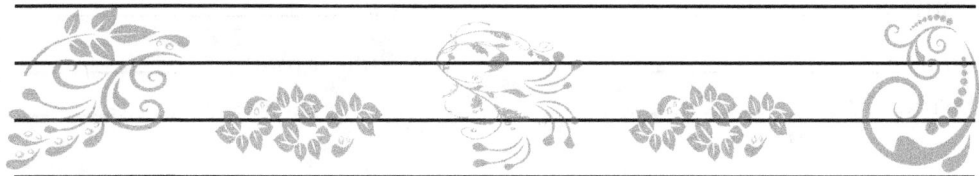

Address Book

name : _____
address : _____
_____
_____
mobile 1 #: _____
mobile 2 #: _____
work #: _____
home #: _____
email : _____
birthday : _____

name : _____
address : _____
_____
_____
mobile 1 #: _____
mobile 2 #: _____
work #: _____
home #: _____
email : _____
birthday : _____

name : _____
address : _____
_____
_____
mobile 1 #: _____
mobile 2 #: _____
work #: _____
home #: _____
email : _____
birthday : _____

name : _____
address : _____
_____
_____
mobile 1 #: _____
mobile 2 #: _____
work #: _____
home #: _____
email : _____
birthday : _____

name : _____
address : _____
_____
_____
mobile 1 #: _____
mobile 2 #: _____
work #: _____
home #: _____
email : _____
birthday : _____

name : _____
address : _____
_____
_____
mobile 1 #: _____
mobile 2 #: _____
work #: _____
home #: _____
email : _____
birthday : _____

 # journal

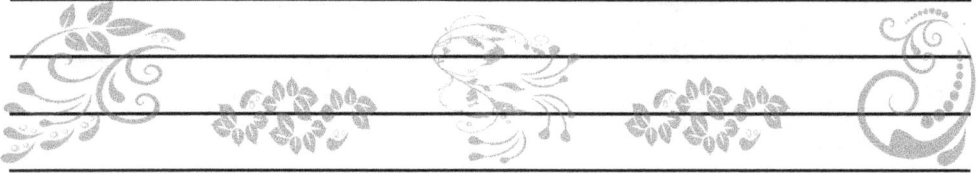

Address Book

name : _____
address : _____
_____
_____
mobile 1 #: _____
mobile 2 #: _____
work #: _____
home #: _____
email : _____
birthday : _____

name : _____
address : _____
_____
_____
mobile 1 #: _____
mobile 2 #: _____
work #: _____
home #: _____
email : _____
birthday : _____

name : _____
address : _____
_____
_____
mobile 1 #: _____
mobile 2 #: _____
work #: _____
home #: _____
email : _____
birthday : _____

name : _____
address : _____
_____
_____
mobile 1 #: _____
mobile 2 #: _____
work #: _____
home #: _____
email : _____
birthday : _____

name : _____
address : _____
_____
_____
mobile 1 #: _____
mobile 2 #: _____
work #: _____
home #: _____
email : _____
birthday : _____

name : _____
address : _____
_____
_____
mobile 1 #: _____
mobile 2 #: _____
work #: _____
home #: _____
email : _____
birthday : _____

journal

Address Book

name : _____
address : _____
_____
_____
mobile 1 #: _____
mobile 2 #: _____
work #: _____
home #: _____
email :_____
birthday : _____

name : _____
address : _____
_____
_____
mobile 1 #: _____
mobile 2 #: _____
work #: _____
home #: _____
email :_____
birthday : _____

name : _____
address : _____
_____
_____
mobile 1 #: _____
mobile 2 #: _____
work #: _____
home #: _____
email :_____
birthday : _____

name : _____
address : _____
_____
_____
mobile 1 #: _____
mobile 2 #: _____
work #: _____
home #: _____
email :_____
birthday : _____

name : _____
address : _____
_____
_____
mobile 1 #: _____
mobile 2 #: _____
work #: _____
home #: _____
email :_____
birthday : _____

name : _____
address : _____
_____
_____
mobile 1 #: _____
mobile 2 #: _____
work #: _____
home #: _____
email : _____
birthday : _____

journal

Address Book

name : _____
address : _____
_____
_____
mobile 1 #: _____
mobile 2 #: _____
work #: _____
home #: _____
email :_____
birthday : _____

name : _____
address : _____
_____
_____
mobile 1 #: _____
mobile 2 #: _____
work #: _____
home #: _____
email :_____
birthday : _____

name : _____
address : _____
_____
_____
mobile 1 #: _____
mobile 2 #: _____
work #: _____
home #: _____
email :_____
birthday : _____

name : _____
address : _____
_____
_____
mobile 1 #: _____
mobile 2 #: _____
work #: _____
home #: _____
email :_____
birthday : _____

name : _____
address : _____
_____
_____
mobile 1 #: _____
mobile 2 #: _____
work #: _____
home #: _____
email :_____
birthday : _____

name : _____
address : _____
_____
_____
mobile 1 #: _____
mobile 2 #: _____
work #: _____
home #: _____
email :_____
birthday : _____

 journal

Address Book

name : _____
address : _____
_____
_____
mobile 1 #: _____
mobile 2 #: _____
work #: _____
home #: _____
email : _____
birthday : _____

name : _____
address : _____
_____
_____
mobile 1 #: _____
mobile 2 #: _____
work #: _____
home #: _____
email : _____
birthday : _____

name : _____
address : _____
_____
_____
mobile 1 #: _____
mobile 2 #: _____
work #: _____
home #: _____
email : _____
birthday : _____

name : _____
address : _____
_____
_____
mobile 1 #: _____
mobile 2 #: _____
work #: _____
home #: _____
email : _____
birthday : _____

name : _____
address : _____
_____
_____
mobile 1 #: _____
mobile 2 #: _____
work #: _____
home #: _____
email : _____
birthday : _____

name : _____
address : _____
_____
_____
mobile 1 #: _____
mobile 2 #: _____
work #: _____
home #: _____
email : _____
birthday : _____

 journal

Address Book

name : _____
address : _____
_____
_____
mobile 1 #: _____
mobile 2 #: _____
work #: _____
home #: _____
email : _____
birthday : _____

name : _____
address : _____
_____
_____
mobile 1 #: _____
mobile 2 #: _____
work #: _____
home #: _____
email : _____
birthday : _____

name : _____
address : _____
_____
_____
mobile 1 #: _____
mobile 2 #: _____
work #: _____
home #: _____
email : _____
birthday : _____

name : _____
address : _____
_____
_____
mobile 1 #: _____
mobile 2 #: _____
work #: _____
home #: _____
email : _____
birthday : _____

name : _____
address : _____
_____
_____
mobile 1 #: _____
mobile 2 #: _____
work #: _____
home #: _____
email : _____
birthday : _____

name : _____
address : _____
_____
_____
mobile 1 #: _____
mobile 2 #: _____
work #: _____
home #: _____
email : _____
birthday : _____

 journal

Address Book

name : _____
address : _____
_____
_____
mobile 1 #: _____
mobile 2 #: _____
work #: _____
home #: _____
email : _____
birthday : _____

name : _____
address : _____
_____
_____
mobile 1 #: _____
mobile 2 #: _____
work #: _____
home #: _____
email : _____
birthday : _____

name : _____
address : _____
_____
_____
mobile 1 #: _____
mobile 2 #: _____
work #: _____
home #: _____
email : _____
birthday : _____

name : _____
address : _____
_____
_____
mobile 1 #: _____
mobile 2 #: _____
work #: _____
home #: _____
email : _____
birthday : _____

name : _____
address : _____
_____
_____
mobile 1 #: _____
mobile 2 #: _____
work #: _____
home #: _____
email : _____
birthday : _____

name : _____
address : _____
_____
_____
mobile 1 #: _____
mobile 2 #: _____
work #: _____
home #: _____
email : _____
birthday : _____

 journal

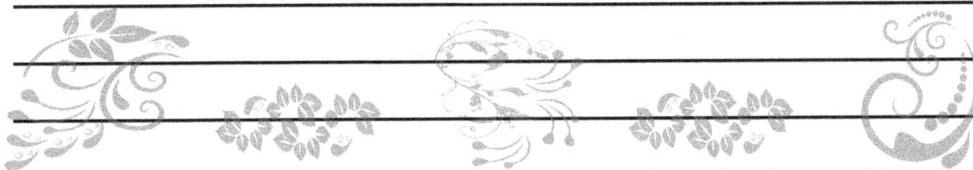

Address Book

name : _____
address : _____
_____
_____
mobile 1 #: _____
mobile 2 #: _____
work #: _____
home #: _____
email : _____
birthday : _____

name : _____
address : _____
_____
_____
mobile 1 #: _____
mobile 2 #: _____
work #: _____
home #: _____
email : _____
birthday : _____

name : _____
address : _____
_____
_____
mobile 1 #: _____
mobile 2 #: _____
work #: _____
home #: _____
email : _____
birthday : _____

name : _____
address : _____
_____
_____
mobile 1 #: _____
mobile 2 #: _____
work #: _____
home #: _____
email : _____
birthday : _____

name : _____
address : _____
_____
_____
mobile 1 #: _____
mobile 2 #: _____
work #: _____
home #: _____
email : _____
birthday : _____

name : _____
address : _____
_____
_____
mobile 1 #: _____
mobile 2 #: _____
work #: _____
home #: _____
email : _____
birthday : _____

 journal

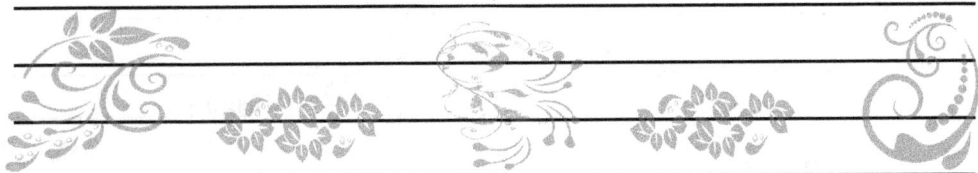

Address Book

name : _____
address : _____
_____
_____
mobile 1 #: _____
mobile 2 #: _____
work #: _____
home #: _____
email : _____
birthday : _____

name : _____
address : _____
_____
_____
mobile 1 #: _____
mobile 2 #: _____
work #: _____
home #: _____
email : _____
birthday : _____

name : _____
address : _____
_____
_____
mobile 1 #: _____
mobile 2 #: _____
work #: _____
home #: _____
email : _____
birthday : _____

name : _____
address : _____
_____
_____
mobile 1 #: _____
mobile 2 #: _____
work #: _____
home #: _____
email : _____
birthday : _____

name : _____
address : _____
_____
_____
mobile 1 #: _____
mobile 2 #: _____
work #: _____
home #: _____
email : _____
birthday : _____

name : _____
address : _____
_____
_____
mobile 1 #: _____
mobile 2 #: _____
work #: _____
home #: _____
email : _____
birthday : _____

 journal

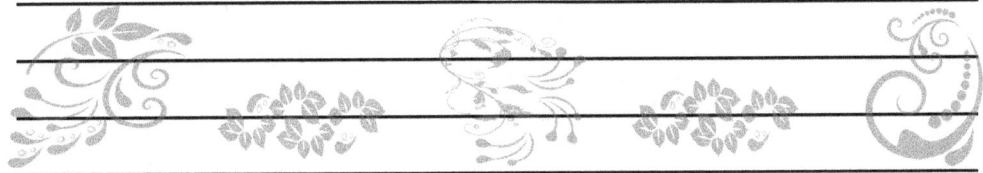

Address Book

name : _____
address : _____
_____
_____
mobile 1 #: _____
mobile 2 #: _____
work #: _____
home #: _____
email : _____
birthday : _____

name : _____
address : _____
_____
_____
mobile 1 #: _____
mobile 2 #: _____
work #: _____
home #: _____
email : _____
birthday : _____

name : _____
address : _____
_____
_____
mobile 1 #: _____
mobile 2 #: _____
work #: _____
home #: _____
email : _____
birthday : _____

name : _____
address : _____
_____
_____
mobile 1 #: _____
mobile 2 #: _____
work #: _____
home #: _____
email : _____
birthday : _____

name : _____
address : _____
_____
_____
mobile 1 #: _____
mobile 2 #: _____
work #: _____
home #: _____
email : _____
birthday : _____

name : _____
address : _____
_____
_____
mobile 1 #: _____
mobile 2 #: _____
work #: _____
home #: _____
email : _____
birthday : _____

 journal

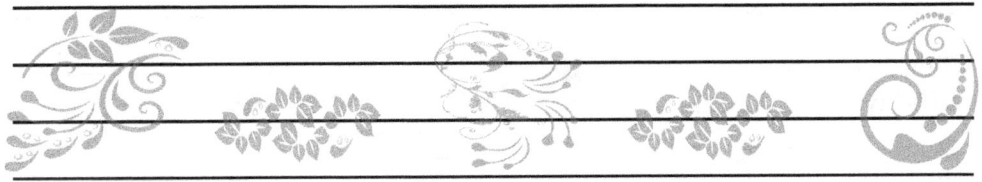

Address Book

name : _____
address : _____
_____
_____
mobile 1 #: _____
mobile 2 #: _____
work #: _____
home #: _____
email : _____
birthday : _____

name : _____
address : _____
_____
_____
mobile 1 #: _____
mobile 2 #: _____
work #: _____
home #: _____
email : _____
birthday : _____

name : _____
address : _____
_____
_____
mobile 1 #: _____
mobile 2 #: _____
work #: _____
home #: _____
email : _____
birthday : _____

name : _____
address : _____
_____
_____
mobile 1 #: _____
mobile 2 #: _____
work #: _____
home #: _____
email : _____
birthday : _____

name : _____
address : _____
_____
_____
mobile 1 #: _____
mobile 2 #: _____
work #: _____
home #: _____
email : _____
birthday : _____

name : _____
address : _____
_____
_____
mobile 1 #: _____
mobile 2 #: _____
work #: _____
home #: _____
email : _____
birthday : _____

 journal

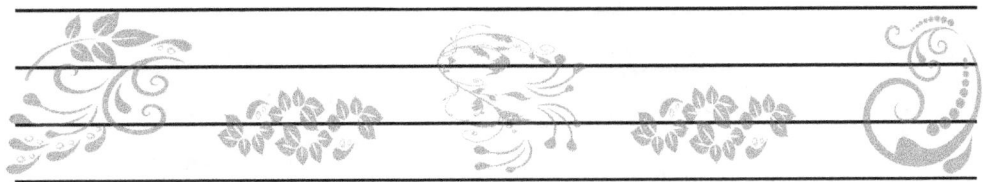

Address Book

name : _____
address : _____
_____
_____
mobile 1 #: _____
mobile 2 #: _____
work #: _____
home #: _____
email : _____
birthday : _____

name : _____
address : _____
_____
_____
mobile 1 #: _____
mobile 2 #: _____
work #: _____
home #: _____
email : _____
birthday : _____

name : _____
address : _____
_____
_____
mobile 1 #: _____
mobile 2 #: _____
work #: _____
home #: _____
email : _____
birthday : _____

name : _____
address : _____
_____
_____
mobile 1 #: _____
mobile 2 #: _____
work #: _____
home #: _____
email : _____
birthday : _____

name : _____
address : _____
_____
_____
mobile 1 #: _____
mobile 2 #: _____
work #: _____
home #: _____
email : _____
birthday : _____

name : _____
address : _____
_____
_____
mobile 1 #: _____
mobile 2 #: _____
work #: _____
home #: _____
email : _____
birthday : _____

 journal

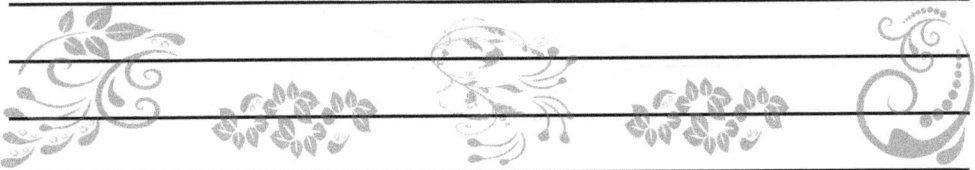

Address Book

name : _____
address : _____
_____
_____
mobile 1 #: _____
mobile 2 #: _____
work #: _____
home #: _____
email : _____
birthday : _____

name : _____
address : _____
_____
_____
mobile 1 #: _____
mobile 2 #: _____
work #: _____
home #: _____
email : _____
birthday : _____

name : _____
address : _____
_____
_____
mobile 1 #: _____
mobile 2 #: _____
work #: _____
home #: _____
email : _____
birthday : _____

name : _____
address : _____
_____
_____
mobile 1 #: _____
mobile 2 #: _____
work #: _____
home #: _____
email : _____
birthday : _____

name : _____
address : _____
_____
_____
mobile 1 #: _____
mobile 2 #: _____
work #: _____
home #: _____
email : _____
birthday : _____

name : _____
address : _____
_____
_____
mobile 1 #: _____
mobile 2 #: _____
work #: _____
home #: _____
email : _____
birthday : _____

journal

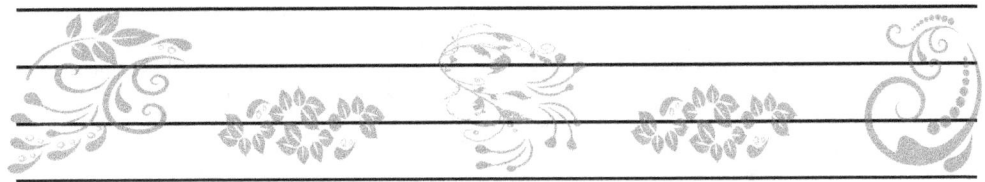

Address Book

name : _____
address : _____
_____
_____
mobile 1 #: _____
mobile 2 #: _____
work #: _____
home #: _____
email : _____
birthday : _____

name : _____
address : _____
_____
_____
mobile 1 #: _____
mobile 2 #: _____
work #: _____
home #: _____
email : _____
birthday : _____

name : _____
address : _____
_____
_____
mobile 1 #: _____
mobile 2 #: _____
work #: _____
home #: _____
email : _____
birthday : _____

name : _____
address : _____
_____
_____
mobile 1 #: _____
mobile 2 #: _____
work #: _____
home #: _____
email : _____
birthday : _____

name : _____
address : _____
_____
_____
mobile 1 #: _____
mobile 2 #: _____
work #: _____
home #: _____
email : _____
birthday : _____

name : _____
address : _____
_____
_____
mobile 1 #: _____
mobile 2 #: _____
work #: _____
home #: _____
email : _____
birthday : _____

journal

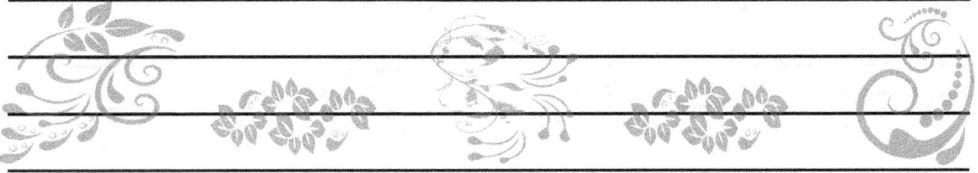

Address Book

name : _____
address : _____
_____
_____
mobile 1 #: _____
mobile 2 #: _____
work #: _____
home #: _____
email :_____
birthday : _____

name : _____
address : _____
_____
_____
mobile 1 #: _____
mobile 2 #: _____
work #: _____
home #: _____
email :_____
birthday : _____

name : _____
address : _____
_____
_____
mobile 1 #: _____
mobile 2 #: _____
work #: _____
home #: _____
email :_____
birthday : _____

name : _____
address : _____
_____
_____
mobile 1 #: _____
mobile 2 #: _____
work #: _____
home #: _____
email :_____
birthday : _____

name : _____
address : _____
_____
_____
mobile 1 #: _____
mobile 2 #: _____
work #: _____
home #: _____
email :_____
birthday : _____

name : _____
address : _____
_____
_____
mobile 1 #: _____
mobile 2 #: _____
work #: _____
home #: _____
email :_____
birthday : _____

 journal

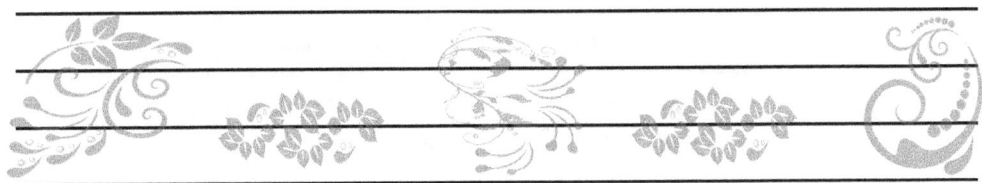

Address Book

name : _____
address : _____
_____
_____
mobile 1 #: _____
mobile 2 #: _____
work #: _____
home #: _____
email :_____
birthday : _____

name : _____
address : _____
_____
_____
mobile 1 #: _____
mobile 2 #: _____
work #: _____
home #: _____
email :_____
birthday : _____

name : _____
address : _____
_____
_____
mobile 1 #: _____
mobile 2 #: _____
work #: _____
home #: _____
email :_____
birthday : _____

name : _____
address : _____
_____
_____
mobile 1 #: _____
mobile 2 #: _____
work #: _____
home #: _____
email :_____
birthday : _____

name : _____
address : _____
_____
_____
mobile 1 #: _____
mobile 2 #: _____
work #: _____
home #: _____
email :_____
birthday : _____

name : _____
address : _____
_____
_____
mobile 1 #: _____
mobile 2 #: _____
work #: _____
home #: _____
email :_____
birthday : _____

 journal

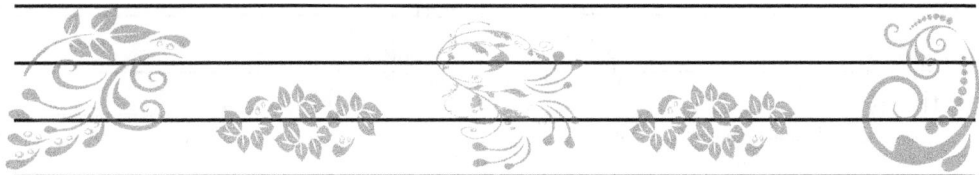

Address Book

name : _____
address : _____
_____
_____
mobile 1 #: _____
mobile 2 #: _____
work #: _____
home #: _____
email : _____
birthday : _____

name : _____
address : _____
_____
_____
mobile 1 #: _____
mobile 2 #: _____
work #: _____
home #: _____
email : _____
birthday : _____

name : _____
address : _____
_____
_____
mobile 1 #: _____
mobile 2 #: _____
work #: _____
home #: _____
email : _____
birthday : _____

name : _____
address : _____
_____
_____
mobile 1 #: _____
mobile 2 #: _____
work #: _____
home #: _____
email : _____
birthday : _____

name : _____
address : _____
_____
_____
mobile 1 #: _____
mobile 2 #: _____
work #: _____
home #: _____
email : _____
birthday : _____

name : _____
address : _____
_____
_____
mobile 1 #: _____
mobile 2 #: _____
work #: _____
home #: _____
email : _____
birthday : _____

 journal

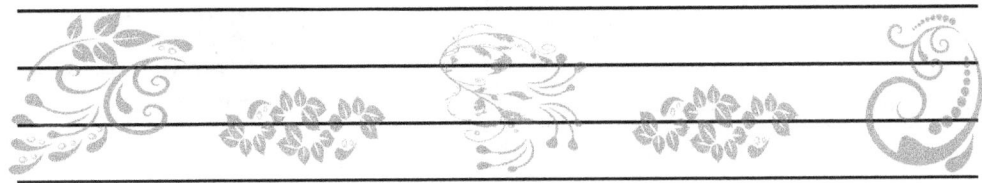

Address Book

name : _____
address : _____
_____
_____
mobile 1 #: _____
mobile 2 #: _____
work #: _____
home #: _____
email :_____
birthday : _____

name : _____
address : _____
_____
_____
mobile 1 #: _____
mobile 2 #: _____
work #: _____
home #: _____
email :_____
birthday : _____

name : _____
address : _____
_____
_____
mobile 1 #: _____
mobile 2 #: _____
work #: _____
home #: _____
email :_____
birthday : _____

name : _____
address : _____
_____
_____
mobile 1 #: _____
mobile 2 #: _____
work #: _____
home #: _____
email :_____
birthday : _____

name : _____
address : _____
_____
_____
mobile 1 #: _____
mobile 2 #: _____
work #: _____
home #: _____
email :_____
birthday : _____

name : _____
address : _____
_____
_____
mobile 1 #: _____
mobile 2 #: _____
work #: _____
home #: _____
email :_____
birthday : _____

 journal

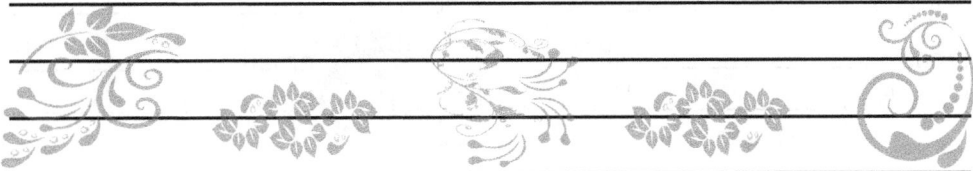

Address Book

name : _____
address : _____
_____
_____
mobile 1 #: _____
mobile 2 #: _____
work #: _____
home #: _____
email :_____
birthday : _____

name : _____
address : _____
_____
_____
mobile 1 #: _____
mobile 2 #: _____
work #: _____
home #: _____
email :_____
birthday : _____

name : _____
address : _____
_____
_____
mobile 1 #: _____
mobile 2 #: _____
work #: _____
home #: _____
email :_____
birthday : _____

name : _____
address : _____
_____
_____
mobile 1 #: _____
mobile 2 #: _____
work #: _____
home #: _____
email :_____
birthday : _____

name : _____
address : _____
_____
_____
mobile 1 #: _____
mobile 2 #: _____
work #: _____
home #: _____
email :_____
birthday : _____

name : _____
address : _____
_____
_____
mobile 1 #: _____
mobile 2 #: _____
work #: _____
home #: _____
email :_____
birthday : _____

 journal

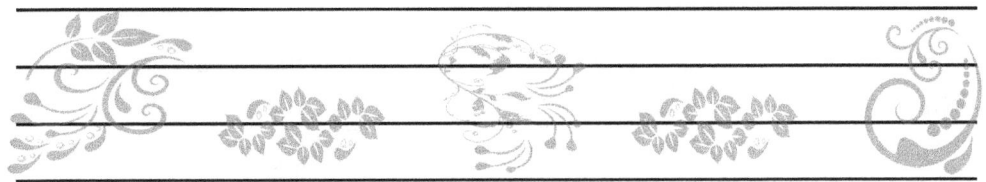

Address Book

name : _____
address : _____
_____
_____
mobile 1 #: _____
mobile 2 #: _____
work #: _____
home #: _____
email :_____
birthday : _____

name : _____
address : _____
_____
_____
mobile 1 #: _____
mobile 2 #: _____
work #: _____
home #: _____
email :_____
birthday : _____

name : _____
address : _____
_____
_____
mobile 1 #: _____
mobile 2 #: _____
work #: _____
home #: _____
email :_____
birthday : _____

name : _____
address : _____
_____
_____
mobile 1 #: _____
mobile 2 #: _____
work #: _____
home #: _____
email :_____
birthday : _____

name : _____
address : _____
_____
_____
mobile 1 #: _____
mobile 2 #: _____
work #: _____
home #: _____
email :_____
birthday : _____

name : _____
address : _____
_____
_____
mobile 1 #: _____
mobile 2 #: _____
work #: _____
home #: _____
email :_____
birthday : _____

 journal

Address Book

name : _____
address : _____
_____
_____
mobile 1 #: _____
mobile 2 #: _____
work #: _____
home #: _____
email : _____
birthday : _____

name : _____
address : _____
_____
_____
mobile 1 #: _____
mobile 2 #: _____
work #: _____
home #: _____
email : _____
birthday : _____

name : _____
address : _____
_____
_____
mobile 1 #: _____
mobile 2 #: _____
work #: _____
home #: _____
email : _____
birthday : _____

name : _____
address : _____
_____
_____
mobile 1 #: _____
mobile 2 #: _____
work #: _____
home #: _____
email : _____
birthday : _____

name : _____
address : _____
_____
_____
mobile 1 #: _____
mobile 2 #: _____
work #: _____
home #: _____
email : _____
birthday : _____

name : _____
address : _____
_____
_____
mobile 1 #: _____
mobile 2 #: _____
work #: _____
home #: _____
email : _____
birthday : _____

 journal

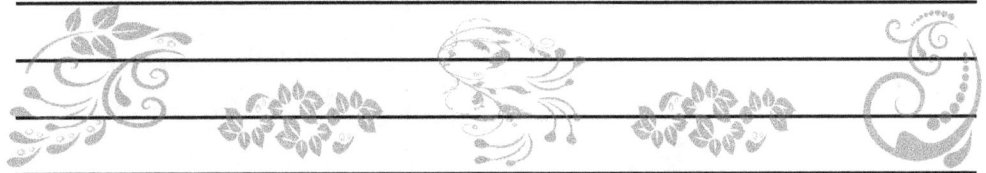

Address Book

name : _____
address : _____
_____
_____
mobile 1 #: _____
mobile 2 #: _____
work #: _____
home #: _____
email : _____
birthday : _____

name : _____
address : _____
_____
_____
mobile 1 #: _____
mobile 2 #: _____
work #: _____
home #: _____
email : _____
birthday : _____

name : _____
address : _____
_____
_____
mobile 1 #: _____
mobile 2 #: _____
work #: _____
home #: _____
email : _____
birthday : _____

name : _____
address : _____
_____
_____
mobile 1 #: _____
mobile 2 #: _____
work #: _____
home #: _____
email : _____
birthday : _____

name : _____
address : _____
_____
_____
mobile 1 #: _____
mobile 2 #: _____
work #: _____
home #: _____
email : _____
birthday : _____

name : _____
address : _____
_____
_____
mobile 1 #: _____
mobile 2 #: _____
work #: _____
home #: _____
email : _____
birthday : _____

 journal

Address Book

name : _____
address : _____
_____
_____
mobile 1 #: _____
mobile 2 #: _____
work #: _____
home #: _____
email : _____
birthday : _____

name : _____
address : _____
_____
_____
mobile 1 #: _____
mobile 2 #: _____
work #: _____
home #: _____
email : _____
birthday : _____

name : _____
address : _____
_____
_____
mobile 1 #: _____
mobile 2 #: _____
work #: _____
home #: _____
email : _____
birthday : _____

name : _____
address : _____
_____
_____
mobile 1 #: _____
mobile 2 #: _____
work #: _____
home #: _____
email : _____
birthday : _____

name : _____
address : _____
_____
_____
mobile 1 #: _____
mobile 2 #: _____
work #: _____
home #: _____
email : _____
birthday : _____

name : _____
address : _____
_____
_____
mobile 1 #: _____
mobile 2 #: _____
work #: _____
home #: _____
email : _____
birthday : _____

 journal

Address Book

name : _____
address : _____
_____
_____
mobile 1 #: _____
mobile 2 #: _____
work #: _____
home #: _____
email : _____
birthday : _____

name : _____
address : _____
_____
_____
mobile 1 #: _____
mobile 2 #: _____
work #: _____
home #: _____
email : _____
birthday : _____

name : _____
address : _____
_____
_____
mobile 1 #: _____
mobile 2 #: _____
work #: _____
home #: _____
email : _____
birthday : _____

name : _____
address : _____
_____
_____
mobile 1 #: _____
mobile 2 #: _____
work #: _____
home #: _____
email : _____
birthday : _____

name : _____
address : _____
_____
_____
mobile 1 #: _____
mobile 2 #: _____
work #: _____
home #: _____
email : _____
birthday : _____

name : _____
address : _____
_____
_____
mobile 1 #: _____
mobile 2 #: _____
work #: _____
home #: _____
email : _____
birthday : _____

 journal

www.ingramcontent.com/pod-product-compliance
Lightning Source LLC
Chambersburg PA
CBHW081337090426
42737CB00017B/3177